T0381337

Easter

Written and Illustrated by
Gwenn Huot

To order additional copies of this book, contact:
Xlibris
844-714-8691
www.Xlibris.com
Orders@Xlibris.com

ISBN: Softcover   978-1-4363-6842-1
        EBook   978-1-6641-4935-9

Print information available on the last page

Rev. date: 12/19/2020

What's the big deal about Easter? Well, ...

One sunny afternoon, Jen borrowed her brother Todd's teddy bear and decided to take it outside to play with, without asking. She knew she wasn't supposed to.

Jen's brother, Todd, had kept that bear from when he was little. Todd's grandmother had given it to him so it was special to him.

Jen took the teddy bear down by the stream. She put the bear down just for a minute. When she turned around, she started to cry. The stream had taken away the bear, and it was gone!

When Todd found out what his little sister did, he said he hated her and was very mad. Jen started to cry.

Todd and Jen decided to follow the river to see if they could find the bear.

After about an hour of floating down the creek, and a whole lot of arguing, they came upon a crowd. There were three men carrying crosses on their shoulders and everyone was shouting.

Todd asked someone what these men had done. The man in the crowd told them that two of these men were thieves, and one of them, Jesus, claims to be the son of God.

Todd asks the man in the crowd, "How do you know if he really is the son of God?" The man answered, "He has healed all kinds of men and He has told people about God and His love."

Todd asked the man "If He is the son of God, then why can't He get himself off of the cross?" The man did not know.

Jesus must have a reason. "I do know he claims to come back to live in three days."

Three days! The two children paddled all the way home.

What a story they had to tell their parents.

Todd was still angry with Jen
for losing his teddy bear, that
they never did find. Todd and
Jen had a hard time sleeping,
but eventually they dozed off.

Three days later, there was a knock at their door. There was a man standing at the door with Todd's teddy bear. Todd's eyes lit up. "Thank you, sir!"

When Todd and Jen looked up at the man, they didn't know what to say. Todd saw the holes in His hands, as He handed him the teddy bear, and he knew right away, He was God's son, Jesus, the same man they saw nailed to the cross.

Jesus' eyes were full of love. They asked Him why He had to die on the cross, and why He came back.

Jesus replied, "A long time ago, Adam and Eve broke a promise to God, my Father. They ate from the tree of good and evil. A sacrifice had to be made to mend or fix that promise. When Adam and Eve ate the forbidden fruit, it made them not worthy to see God.

My dying on the cross made the Holy Spirit available to all of us to help us obey God's Law.

I love you so much that I sacrificed myself to make you worthy to be with God again.

18

Todd looked at Jen. "If Jesus can give His life for us to be able to go to Heaven, then I should be able to forgive you for taking my teddy bear."

The End

(footnote)

Hebrews 9:27 & 28:

We die only once and then we are judged, so Christ died only once to take away the sins of many people. When He comes again, it will not be to take away sin. He will come to save everyone who is waiting for Him.

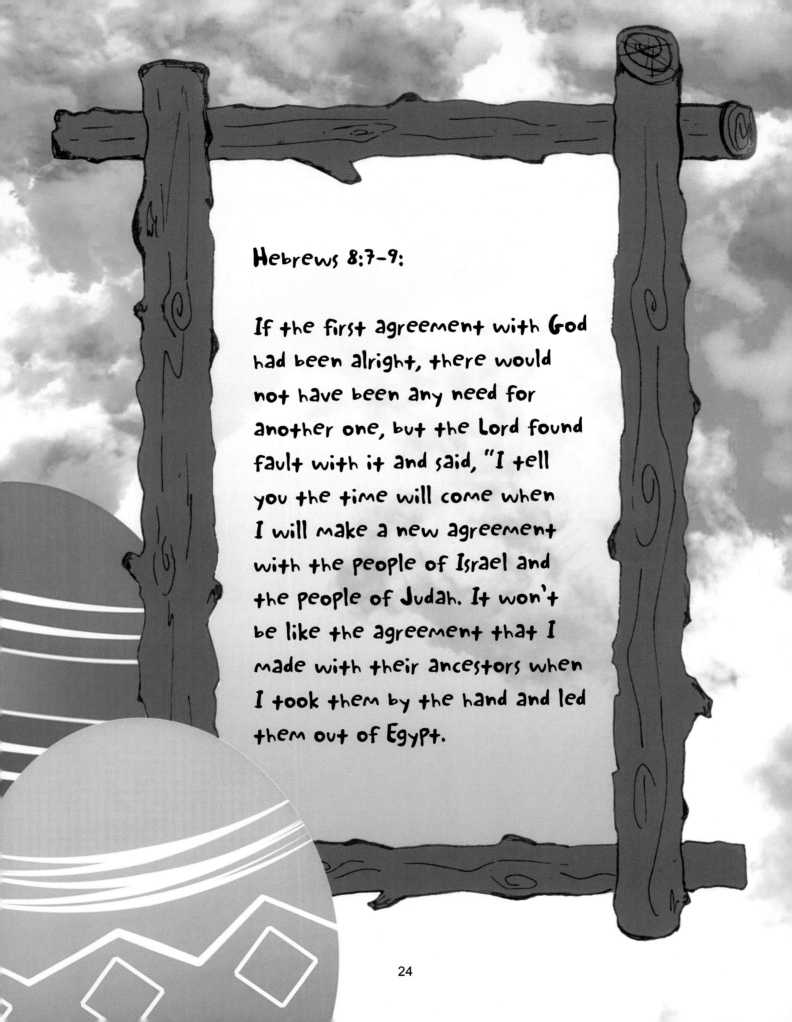

Hebrews 8:7-9:

If the first agreement with God had been alright, there would not have been any need for another one, but the Lord found fault with it and said, "I tell you the time will come when I will make a new agreement with the people of Israel and the people of Judah. It won't be like the agreement that I made with their ancestors when I took them by the hand and led them out of Egypt.

Printed in the United States
By Bookmasters